Cup

of

Fire

---

poems

Marlaina
Donato

Cup of Fire/Marlaina Donato
Blairstown, New Jersey: Ekstasis Multimedia, LLC, 2013
Ekstasis Multimedia: www.booksandbrush.net

ISBN-13: 978-0615818610
ISBN-10: 0615818617

Photography, art, and design: Marlaina Donato

Ekstasis Multimedia
Blairstown, New Jersey

For J.C.D., "Beloved who is the first…."

Contents

I: Thunder's Edge......5

II: Ember Nights......27

III: Dark Moon, Deep Kiss......49

IV: Drinking the Storm......68

V: Silk and Thorns.....90

VI: Breath of Jasmine.....110

VII: Bitter Fruit......129

VIII: Last Touch......156

———————

Index to First Lines......181

About the Author......187

Thunder's Edge

Pomegranate

Desire like an open pomegranate

Rapture like cold morning water

Drawn up from the well of night

Beauty dappled and winged

Out of the cocoon of want

Desire abundant and for the taking

Desire not without price or struggle

As the explosion unearths the gold

As the blade yields the nectar

So too this ecstasy

Not Yet Found

Where October drifts by

In a crimson veil,

I listen for a footstep

Inaudible beneath a century of Autumns.

Lover, who would have been

Yet forever will be,

I look across the barren plain of time,

Hungry to hear your whisper

In the falling leaves,

The dying dream of another year's end.

I turn from October's fevered cheek

To discover your eyes

In the gray ghost-rains of the night,

The smoke of far-away fires,

The moon's silver breath

Upon the brow of the waters.

Longing for eyes once lost

Yet never found,

Love that could have been

Yet always has been,

Lover whose gray eyes overstep centuries to

wash my soul

Of its dark seasons.

Gray-eyed rain, wash my dreams tonight,

Dreams that can never be

Yet, forever, will be…

Salt

Our bodies wear the waves,

Desire buoyant upon the tides;

We thunder

Hunger

Toward home.

You taste like the tides

And my tenth summer

When the sea left its salt in my soul;

Tenth summer, dark waves whitened

On midnight,

I wondered what was within

The sea's wild and wailing heart.

It was you,

Dark and wild and waiting…

It was this ecstasy, this letting go

Of the bottom,

Becoming you, dissolution.

Blue Smoke Morning

Blue smoke morning

Moonstone river, opal city

Hiding us

From who we are out there

In here, only the essentials:

Books and a bed

And a hunger to match the two

And on the wall, a mural of our

On again-off again

In here, room for all the selves

Too numerous for out there

Come back to bed, my Hindu god

With eight arms to hold me

Eight arms to hold the eight of me

Without explanation

Eight arms and incense soul

To love me to silence

Love me home again

Daybreak

Sixteen seasons of cold and darkness

Waiting for a flicker of dawn

From your eyes

Sixteen seasons of famine and drought

Waiting for this morning

This heat, this sun

Heart finally drinking the light

Recognition

Morning crowded with travelers

Only us, only us

And a thousand birds

Singing in your eyes

Amaryllis

You drink the night from my body;

Which is deeper,

Your thirst or my thawing?

Only ecstasy knows the depth

Of this well,

Ecstasy pulled back like scarlet petals

In the urgency of blooming.

Only a flower understands this opening…

I am a hundred doors opening,

A woman birthing, unearthing fire,

Amaryllis unfurling.

Only love knows

The famine of this fulfillment.

I am a hundred rivers thirsting

A woman birthing, unearthing fire,

Amaryllis unfurling.

You drink the night from my body;

Only dawn knows

The sacrifice of this surrender.

I am a hundred mornings rising,

A woman birthing, unearthing fire,

Amaryllis unfurling.

Matches

Heart famished

Feast and sustenance granted

Yet hunger rages

What more could possibly be given

Heart playing with matches

Burning the hours

Spoiled, greedy child

Deaf to discipline

Yet so fragile

Shivering in your corner of need

Destiny

I look into eyes and remember

A forgotten mile,

A heart's unexpected turn

On the way to this morning…

One goodbye less, one step further

And I would have missed forever.

Poison

I would die for you,

Die so you can live in this heart,

This heart that shuts you

In its tower of secrets.

I feed you shadow

And quench you with shame

Until you are fat with emptiness.

I would die for you,

Die so you can live in this fire,

This fire that burns your myrrh

To the gods,

Any god what would

Grant me your touch.

I would die for you,

Not knowing I already have,

A million selves

In the grave of your hands,

And you are now eternal,

Immortal

On the poison of this ambrosia.

Visitation

I feel the cloak of your arms

Comfort me through the years,

The hours that drag their feet

Like stubborn children,

Moments that fly into a lost forever.

Take me with you into the storm

And let me taste thunder unafraid.

I open the secrets of my soul,

This fragile box of flesh

In which they are encased.

I am young, but the anchor of time

Weighs upon the wings of youth;

Yet tonight, I own the skies

And soar against your wilderness.

This night will remain

A shimmering pearl of memory

Among the ashes of a life.

In the long,

Idle eternities of our desperation,

Love visited us.

Oasis

You began a drop of rain,

A whisper of wet;

You are now a storm,

Thunder in my blood.

I began a desert,

A shadow of thirst;

I am now an oasis,

A garden

Should you hunger.

The Dancer

You writhe in the dance,

A small universe against the floor.

I watch you and wrestle with your beauty,

muscle and bone,

Hungry to be the ground beneath you,

To be cold and indifferent,

Unreachable and silent

Beneath your small hands,

Hands that could split

My soul in two…

Hungry to be blind and numb

To your open thighs

And the Eden between.

Beautiful universe,

I watch you and tremble inside

The muscle and the bone,

On the edge of flood.

Now I know

A gesture could create a world

And beauty so untouchable,

A river of whispered prayer.

Beautiful dancer,

I kneel at your Shiva-soul

And bathe in the Ganges of my tears.

March

We take the path along the river,

Chopping through half-melted snow

And dark chocolate mud.

Our boots crunch and slosh

Over the iron bridge

With the Pollack graffiti,

Past the wetland and sleeping frogs,

Toward the waterfall's silver thunder.

Our shadows pause

Every few hundred feet

Against the day's shattered gold.

The sky is so blue it hurts my eyes,

And the earth pulses

Beneath our boot soles.

Shield me even from this beauty,

In the circle of your arms,

Against your neck;

Hold me at the thunder's edge.

Beloved, hold me

At the rim of the world

As I hold the song of the river

That is your heart

Now beating for me, for me

On this day

Of shattered gold and cascading silver.

Ember Nights

Arrival

Twilight shakes blue petals

From her hair,

And the moon scatters

Her broken pearls over the river.

The hours dress in their finery

As I reach into the twilight

And pluck a star

To wear as a trinket;

My soul puts on the party gown

Never worn,

And all of night celebrates

Your coming.

Now That You Are Gone

You are so much nearer to me now,

Now that you are gone;

How easily I can grasp your hand

From the stars

When once, I had to reach eons,

Even when I was in your embrace.

I love you more now,

Now that I no longer love you;

My thoughts return to you

With such quality, such feeling

Now that those thoughts occur

Occasionally rather than continually.

As autumn comes back,

I remember you

Even more vividly than those times

Actually spent with you.

I see you everywhere

Now that you are no longer here

Obstructing my vision.

How much more passion

I have for you

Now that my heart is cold.

I love you more now,

Now that I no longer love you.

Spice Market

Drumming in the streets

Amber woman drenched with dancing

White hem trailing in the dust

Moroccan nights wavering like stars

Kneeling to dine

Men with obsidian eyes

Wearing age or desire

Serpentine paths stenciled

With footprints, signatures

Of countless lives

Heady air haunted

And dizzy with spice

And women's voices

In the procession of passion

I walk alone

Knowing how our bodies would fit

Beneath a moon

More beautiful than youth

Raven

Stranger with eyes like the night,

Eyes of someone I once loved,

Angel with the raven's eyes,

Sit next to me.

Laugh like sudden rain;

Laugh like someone I once loved.

Our nights will never meet,

Yet for this hour

Flood the drought while I memorize

The dark invitation of your hair

And the bronze hands

That would feel like desert wind

Across this barrenness.

Gold Hunger

The fire's gold hunger

Has paled to ember;

I hear the footsteps of the dawn.

You lift your head

From my heart

As we seek one last breath of fire

Before I leave.

Intrusion of daylight

Remains unpardoned

In this eclipse of desire.

Morning waits

For this bitter honey

To fill the thirst

And dark eyes to pale to ember;

Then I scatter into the dawn,

Heart a startled bird

Into the pain of light.

Moon Upon Wave

The sea shimmers in the moon's

Half-empty light.

With each wave's turning

The light flames silver

Then goes out by foam.

With each star's burning

Night dreams on the billows.

At this hour of Love's yearning

My soul

Walks

With your soul.

Lost long,

Long lost,

I reach

Love's earning.

As moon presses upon wave,

I am pressed to you,

Breathless, deathless

In Love's learning.

Burn

In the wake of burning,

You turn to me in the moonlight,

Your hair a flame in the darkness.

You smile a smile only I know,

Only my body knows…

So pure it lives but a second,

A drop of snow put out by my touch.

Winter night, playing my six string,

Fingers against steel strings

Giving voice to hollow heart of wood.

Hands tire with song, remembering

Making love to you until the burn.

First Night

This night, a leaf in amber

Your beauty imprisoned in memory

Voices of the stars between our bodies

My lips bruised from your hunger

First night

Wrapped in your fire

First light

Morning trembling with memories

Your name, first word

Unspoken, unheard

Absence of pain

Beautiful stain

Of bliss

Having loved you

These hands now holy

Peeling an apple as if the first

First thing tasted since your kiss

Tasting, not wasting

A breath of this

Sweetness

The Flower's Rage

Sleep, savior to the wound,

Tempers the slow hunger of nights,

But what blunts the edge of day,

The slow hunger of the day?

The light cuts with truth:

I am not your lover.

I am not your blood.

I am not your friend,

Not even your enemy.

But a flower crushed

Beneath your step,

A flower

That once longed for

Recognition

From sightless eyes,

Dreamed of being spared

Against your breast.

Could you ever know

The flower's worth

Or the flower's rage...

The moon knows,

Bleeding fire

When the soul

Is an empty cup

Never to be filled again

With the light

That hesitates

On your brow

Before igniting dark eyes.

The gnarled pine knows,

Stenciled in scars

Against the dusk,

Young moon

Climbing its branches;

This twisted dancer knows,

Imprisoned in futile grace.

This heart knows,

This hard, rocky earth

Upturned, ripped, softened,

And opened to receive the seed.

Days of long sun

And rains of grief

Until succulence and swollen sweetness;

A million lifetimes beating

Within its labor

Only to come to

The end of the season

To find the harvest

Will not be gathered.

There is no hunger to receive,

No waiting mouth,

No parted lips

Leaning toward fulfillment,

No emptiness striving

For completion.

You are dead

Yet among the living,

Pulsing with beauty and elusion,

A wave dissolved at first touch,

A star too far, too cold

For human hands.

Damn you, take me…

Take me

Out of nights of want.

Take me

Into your dark fever.

Take me

Out of solitary flight.

Take me

Into captive infinity.

Take me

Out of destiny.

Take me

Into chance.

Take me out of the war.

Take me

Into the dance.

Burn me

With the ash of the dream

That was you.

Feed me,

Feed me the fruit of your lies.

Sleep, savior to the wound,

Tempers the slow hunger of nights;

But what blunts the edge of day,

The slow hunger of the day?

Night Rain

The rain's cool breath

Disturbs the curtain.

Is it a lover coming to call,

Have you found me,

Lover who burdens me with desire

At this fragile hour?

I have yet to press my longing

To your breast

And drink oblivion from your kiss;

O, pour your soul

Into this hollow hour

With the remembrance of your voice

More beautiful

Than a choir of angels drifting

Through the rain.

Hold my quivering life,

Its light and shadow,

The silk and the thorns,

And I will be for you

What the sheath is to the sabre,

And I will be the curtain

That moves to your breath

For an eon of nights.

Dark Moon, Deep Kiss

At an Art Opening

Laughter overflows

In a room crowded with words;

In a blur of conversation,

I am torn between listening

And locating your presence

By the door.

Then your sudden smile, a flower

Opening to my sunlight

…Hello…

Morning

Day emerges

From a cocoon of snow;

Dawn spills over

As we eat your pancakes

By the window.

Your hair is still wild

From the storm of my hands,

And you smell like maple syrup

And love.

Night-Bloom

So this is what it would be like
If Fate had given us a full harvest,
Both of us at evening's turning
Each bringing
The day's experience
For the other to examine;
Exchanging thoughts
After the book is closed,
A slow kiss over burgundy,
A smile antiqued
By a candle's gold,
A brush of hand between words.
But our hearts fell upon thorns;
Our love will not reap orchards,
But a single flower

Born in impossibility,

Each petal a miracle

Awakened in darkness.

This flower

However small,

However fragile,

Is perennial.

Pilgrimage

He moves inside me

Hard rhythm of storm

I move inside him

Soft ocean flame

Undertow and morning sun

In this bed of Eden

We journey to God

A pilgrimage of flesh and prayer

Dance of grace

Dionysos

Along a pathway of moon

We run with new wine in our veins;

We dance, sandaled in visions,

God of the Dark Thirst,

God of the Dark Nirvana,

Find me with eyes

Of amethyst fire

And hair that waves black

As the river.

Fill me with ecstasy

That has never known the sun.

Pain me with joy

That has known suffering.

Entrance me with music

Wilder than your leopards

Crouching in the shadows

With intoxicated eyes.

Anoint me

With your soul's first pressing;

Feed me your kiss of bittersweetness,

Kiss of wine and myrrh…

All days of bright bliss

Are sacrificed for one night

With you,

God of the Dark Thirst,

God of the Dark Nirvana,

Lord of the intrepid seeker

Who seeks you tonight.

Yin/Yang

Your black boots

With a million miles

Branded

Into the soles

My red poet's blouse

With a maze of laces

Your hungry fingers

Have no time for

Your voice, sweet smoke and brandy

Copious with words

Mine,

An E-string on a guitar

Slightly out of tune

Your body,

Light as water

Flowing over

The heavy curve

Of my driftwood

Clothes, voices, bodies

Weaving

Such harmony of opposites

Dark Moon, Deep Kiss

Dark moon, deep kiss

Diving into oceans

Beneath your tongue

Your hair spilling gold

Into my touch

The darkness trembling

Bodies braid then burn

My soul, a naked flame

As you shatter my depths

With bare hands

Cardamom

Reason to ruin, senses drugged

A kiss, a fragrance like fire

Nights like cardamom

Serpentine trance

Blinding seas

Nights like cardamom

This is what they died for

Killed for

Discovered new continents for

Hungered for

One breath of spice

Against the tongue

Wine would never suffice again

After monotony, madness

At any cost

Nights like cardamom

My name burning on your tongue

Whisper more precious than gold

Nights like cardamom

Flowers in the Storm

Night wind

Through the half-open door

Rain and waves, a thousand drums

Scent of flowers in the storm

My body, thawing spring

Rain-soaked with your desire

Ecstasy torrential

Black Denim

Silhouetted against city light

We kiss goodbye

Against a darkened door.

We still have yet to touch

For the first time,

But not yet, not tonight…

Let me sleep alone, content

With only the thought

Of your denim

Against my bare skin.

Ruby Glass

Slow dance to Spanish music

3 a.m. and the air smells like wine

A breath of sea

Through an open window

Candles shivering in ruby glass

Intoxicated by your words

Against my throat

Desire too deep to disturb

Dancing to flamenco guitar

As the wind blows

Our bodies shivering

Like candles in ruby glass

Ember

Mist like ash

Morning sky silver before sun

Maples half burning in October gold

Arms circled in silence

We walk after love

Bodies still pulsing

So alive

We can hear a single leaf

Drift to wet ground

An ember extinguished

Downpour

Wash my soul

In the dark rain of your hair

Rain on this night

Resounding with your silence

Drink these secrets

Beneath my kiss

(Let me have this dream)

Drench me with words

You will never say

(Let me have this dream)

My only wealth

In this night of poverty

Rain Pool

We whisper, afraid a single word

Will startle a heaven of stars

Caught in the dark mirror

Of a rain pool.

You cup your hands

For me to drink,

Your heartbeat tremors in my veins

And in the cool, wet abandon

Of your fingers upon my thirst.

My life, withered

And threadbare by the ages,

Opens and drinks starlight.

Drinking the Storm

Last Day

I imagine myself sitting,

Wearing a purple dress

With an open book

Across my knees

And a maple tree lit with sun

Beyond the porch swing.

O, to die in May

With poetry in my lap

And your smile in my memory.

Envy

First taste of wanting

The flower's opium

First taste of needing

The flower's poison

First taste of hating

The flower's sunlight

First Spring

Our laughter drifts

On a rose-colored wind

As we waltz down an avenue

White-washed with blossoms.

I want to leave this life

Dancing in your arms

When all the world

Is lit with your smile.

The day tries to hold spring

Against its dappled breast

As the aged clutch at memories.

An old woman limps across

Our rejoicing…

No band rests on the spotted left hand;

Widowed hopes sleep

Beneath her withered surface

Of seasons.

She is a gnarled reminder

Of a tree once towering

In the twilight.

Spring returns with blossomed enthusiasm

while she sits

Without a single branch to bloom.

She finds no more purpose in flowers

And keeps her gaze to the North

Where all barren things

And ornate springs

Cease.

Vignettes of April

A child's laughter

Rises above the fountain

Like water spray

As a young woman sits

On the church steps, wind blowing

Her auburn against the sky.

We take our bikes

Through the city,

Wheels scattering

Pink rain of blossoms.

We study stained glass

And speak of angels

With my hand in your back pocket.

Avenues of open flowers

Shouting crimson

As I chase your desire
To the third floor
Memorizing Sunday sun
And April in your eyes.

Short Story

She sits three benches away
With pewter hair and a tweed coat
Carelessly buttoned.
Morning sun breaks through
As we invent her life…
How beautiful she once was
As she carried her sketch book
To meet him between classes;
He would read her
His latest chapter
Over coffee and croissants,
And she'd brush his hair back
To memorize its sunlight.
Through marriage
And three daughters

Only a single painting remained
In an attic of memories
And abandoned quests.

A young man sits across from her
And she suddenly remembers
His face.
Could it be…
For a flicker, she dreams.
No, he would be old now, too.
We stand to go,
Contemplating the end…
She asks him the time
Just to see his eyes,
The same blue without the fire;
No eyes ever burned like his.
We laugh down the street,
Glancing backward.

Instead, the young man perches

On his bike;

She does not glance up.

Will people weave stories

About us someday

When we are old

And could we ever live up to them?

Beginning

Morning, an hour old

Eager and spending light

New arms radiant

This love just born

Every breath the first

Every goodbye the last

Every word a touch

Too beautiful to voice

Genesis

Saffron

I wake to the sound

Of church bells

In the valley

And the scent

Of last night's wine.

The back of his neck,

Just where the waves

Touch the bone,

I inhale the scent

Of earth and bread and honey.

Sunday morning,

With my body

Pressed to his,

I wake to the sound

Of new memories,

Last night's words,

His whisper

Like a feather falling against

The darkness.

We make love to the sunrise

Then walk into a saffron day,

Drunk on gold.

Refuge

In you, new harvest

In me, a soul hollow with rot

In you, heaven's blowing silk

In me, the knee-deep mud of Hell

In you, a table of bread

In me, hunger of a thousand nights

Forgive me for entering

Without knocking

Pardon my heart's unkempt mess

Overlook the torn years

And dirty dreams

Disregard eyes that look too long

And blood-stained hands that cling

Give me a bed and sleep's dark kiss

Give me shelter until morning

Until these bitter winds

Die over the mountains

Triangle

I did not know

One night of fire

Would turn into

A wish for a lifetime

And the years Fate granted

To someone else…

The nights of music,

Children's rooms

Lit with laughter,

And the rose-patterned dishes…

Cappuccino

City dawn, a gray flower unfolding

Orchestra of cars

Day's curtain opening

Spotlight of sun

Morning jazz and your smile

Kiss, languid, endless

Cappuccino getting cold

Tempest

The waves are wild tonight;

Driftwood is testimony.

With broken wings,

Through miles of tempest,

Youth flies back to me

Searching for shelter.

But there is no harbor here

In this heart ravaged by wisdom.

You walk beside me

Holding scattered petals of the years;

Let me look away,

Let me defy their fragrance;

Let me only remember thorns.

Night Jewels

We sat near the street

And you blew into

Your cinnamon tea;

We shared

A chocolate strawberry

Knowing it was a kiss goodbye.

We talked while the wind

Took our laughter

And passing cars blew your words

Against me.

In that light, you gave me your eyes;

You slipped them to me

Like stolen jewels.

We sat near the street

And I denied the coming morning

And its four hundred miles.

In that light, I gave you my heart;

I slipped it to you

In the envelope of my life

If you should ever want it.

Unlocked

Solstice moon, holy and heavy

Over our aching

Hearts like desert flowers

Drinking the storm

During the long drought of my youth

Had I only known

The coming of these rains

Desire ages into love

The last door in my heart

Unlocks and opens

Welcome, my beloved

May you stay a lifetime

Eros

Thou hast pierced me

With thy arrow of light,

O, great prince of love,

And left in my heart

A wound of gold

And took from my eyes

My mortal sight.

Prince of love, where am I to go?

For I have eyes no more;

Thy way is dark, thy wound is deep,

But I am grateful forevermore.

I am blind and hurt,

But both are sweet.

Silk and Thorns

Flicker

He brushes past me,

A quiet comet of light,

His hair is dark earth

And in his sweat, the salt of its soul.

I weave the hours of the day,

Scrubbing the harvest

By a window,

Glancing up to glimpse

His passing,

Noticing the hands

That have known heartwood

And the love of a good woman.

Hours of simmering scents,

Weathered wooden spoon,

And warm bread,

A flicker of longing,

Sampling the thought

Of him,

Eating the dream

Of impossible nights.

Concerto

Our words flutter against the moment,

Hurried streams of laughter.

You in crimson

With your gypsy eyes

And the concerto of light

Playing on your bottom lip

As you speak.

You tell me the finches

Have made a nest in the fern

And the difficulty

Of watering the soil

Without drowning the eggs

Not yet hatched.

But all I can hear

Is the concerto,

Memorized note for note,

Year after year,

With the constancy of finches

Who come back.

The hours burn white and quick;

I see them etched in your skin,

In my hair's silver beginning.

When I was a child I dreamed

Of growing old with you,

Of your heart's ember in mine.

Eons since the dream…

After beating Fate with futile hands,

Surrender.

Our words flutter against the moment

As our tea gets cold

And the finches fuss above our heads.

Blessed, these hours that burn

White and quick

And your face more beautiful

Than memory.

Blessed, this fate

And growing old together;

This way, the only way,

Like learning to water the fern

Without drowning the eggs…

Careful and slow the stream,

Like love long unspoken,

This love, the only love

That can stay.

Invocation

Day of thorns

Soul, barefoot and tired

Shut the door

Invoke sleep with your name

Alone at last

With the thought of you

Reflection

Your child

Will never sleep in my womb,

Child who would be given

Your eyes

And their sweet smile of sadness.

I will never watch him

Become your reflection

Or when I am old tell him

How I loved your hands

Or about the night

You played the piano

By a candle's half-whispered light

While the world was lost in snow

Diamond

With one glimpse of your eyes

My life's dying blooms into living;

The spring bud slain by snow

Bursts into resurrection.

With one glimpse of your eyes

My heart's abyss ascends into light;

The scattered ashes burn

Into phoenix flight.

With one glimpse of your eyes

My life's prison opens into sky;

The stone soul shatters into diamond.

With one glimpse of your eyes

My life's dying blooms into living.

Judas

I have eaten at your table
And filled my emptiness.
My hand has touched yours
In the same bowl.
I have drunk the wine
Of your presence
And hungered for the bread
Of your body.
I would sell salvation
For the silver
Of your passing touch,
And I would deny you
Three times before the dawn.

Flood

Dream me awake
As we lie in your bed.
Your skin is a language
My soul knew before this life,
And the morning rains gold
On this fragile remembering;
Your arms, at last, the harbor.
I empty the years–
The desolate and futile,
The broken and raging years,
Into your vastness.
Infinite sea, I flood into you,
This river of long-aching.
Drink of me,
Take me to your depths

Until I struggle for breath

And the morning pours gold

Over your arms

That have become my eternity.

Impasse

We walk to the rhythm of waves,

Words just out of the reach of pride.

We travelled the depths,

Too sure of breath.

The sun continues to beckon,

Offering beauty of the horizon,

Unaware your heart

Has gone to sleep.

Ghost

On a night that lifts your eyes

To the stars

I will return…

I will be the wind

That blows across your body.

I will be the earth

That cradles your step.

I will be the dream you half remember

When you kiss the dawn

From her mouth.

Fool's Gold

You walked in carrying a memory,

The memory of your eyes

Plucking my gaze like a bird

Into a net;

The memory of your hair

Blowing gold in summer light,

And how I gave the entirety

Of my being

For your small smile across the world.

You walked in carrying

These remnants of us.

Now divided, we speak from

The safe shores of distance.

Morning sun leaves

A breath of bronze in your hair,

And my heart remembers

The value of fool's gold.

Silence resonates

Between the empty canyons

Of our words,

And winds blow through the hollow

Of our abandoned nights.

And I remember;

I remember.

Night Cry

Laughter across the way

Pierces the rain as I wait for sleep,

But tonight, sleep is a stranger.

Three thousand miles of circumstance

Lie between us.

Tonight I know you are not alone,

And sleep is not with you, too.

I sift through possibility

Searching for a sacrifice

That could buy us tomorrow,

But the Fates place no value

On pauper's dreams.

Tonight I know you are not alone,

And sleep is not with you, too.

Someone else holds

The password into tomorrow

With you,

The one who cradles

Your whisper tonight.

Deep River

At dream's end,

My fire will meet you,

Its heat no longer caged.

You will know

The hungers your eyes satiated,

The nights when I screamed

Your name into echo.

Only then, this deep river

Will rage from its ice,

And all the words that dam my throat

Will mute even the song of God.

The First

With my heart's wine outpoured

For careless thirst

And my body's bread

Broken for hollow hunger,

I accept your bed this night.

Against your soul,

I press the soul never given

And the second innocence

That waits at the end of experience.

Lover who is not the first,

Beloved who is last,

Lift my soul's elusive veil,

Beloved, who is first…

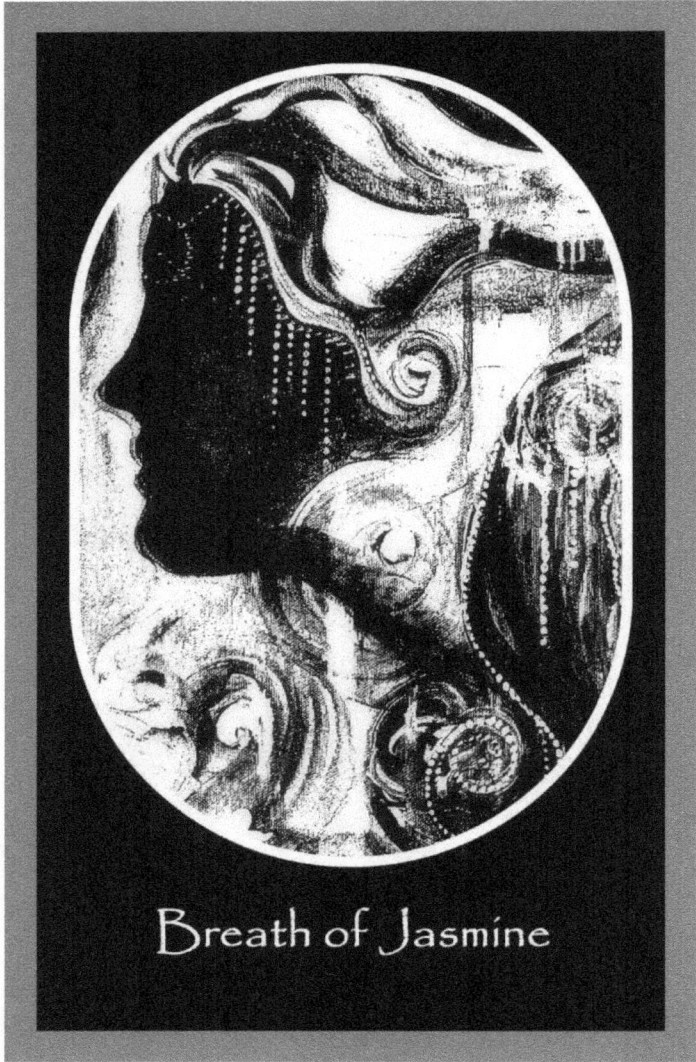

Breath of Jasmine

Divinity

Within each soul

An angel sleeps,

Nestled in oblivion

Until a lover wakes its dreaming.

Tonight your angel

Looked through your eyes

And my angel embraced

Through my arms.

What is love

But the awakening

Of the divinity within ourselves?

First Summer

The day is like warm clay in hand,
Hours molded by nimble fingers
Of conversation,
Matter-of-fact like your ready humor
And my eruptions of laughter.
Our first summer in terra cotta,
Patterned with small joys
Fired in the kiln of this love.
At day's end, fireflies burn like meteors
And we reach for the day's pottery-
Cups of new memory, clear and cool,
Sweet as long-awaited rain
That heals the drought.

Jasmine

A white wall

Wears a necklace of shadows,

Blue thoughts scattered by the sun.

Morning heat pulses like fire;

I watch a carousel of passersby,

Ecru and scarlet.

Your words are the only breeze

Wafting like jasmine

Over my listening.

Summer burns her last hour

As we sit in the shade

And an old man travels the dust

Murmuring to angels.

Constellations

We sit in your car

With the top down

And collect constellations

In a jar of memories.

Too busy with words,

You miss the gold star

Falling

From heaven's highest shelf.

Your laughter

Catches

In my hair

Like this desert wind,

Blowing

A remnant of youth

Into the jar…

Then another dart of gold

Dancing

Across the sky

As we sit in your car

With the top down,

The night crying stars.

Watercolor

Outside, the wind

Disturbs a kiss of snow.

We embrace by the fire,

Your hands warm with apology.

Day blends with night.

Twilight bleeds into autumn white.

We, too, merge…

Breath rising,

Brown hair blows into black.

We merge…

Hearts drumming.

Scarlet of passion and blue of soul.

Violet unity.

Ode to Sunset

Sunrise,

The virgin of the morn…

Sunset,

The bearer of nightfall…

With love,

A bridge of noon is born.

Beloved sunset, your colors of splendor

Will soon fade and grow old.

Today my rays are youthful

And today my rays are new,

But someday, I will be there with you.

Beloved sunset, your colors of splendor

Will soon fade and grow old,

But how I long to kiss your lips,

Your lips of dusky gold.

Please wait and leave behind

A trail of scarlet light,

And together, we will enter

The starlit night.

Within the Reeds

Wind and reed entwine;

Man and woman embrace.

Idle lake, the sky's looking-glass

Mirrors the wind-scattered heaven…

Upon a stage of summer blue,

Cloud dance.

Initiation

Beneath the night's starry wing

I offer myself.

I am perfumed with your soul,

Soul of amber, breath of jasmine.

Tonight, I will be initiated

Into your Mysteries,

Lover deified by desire.

I enter mortal and will leave immortal.

I will leave adorned

With henna and gold,

Invisible until a wind

Blows my garments

And startles the morning with jasmine.

Beloved

Lover, press my petals to your desire

So I may weep my fragrance

And anoint your divinity.

I drench you with rains

Long withheld…

You drink

As parched earth drinks spring.

I have wandered through

Night's labyrinth

To taste this light-shimmering hour

Shining through the prism

Of your smile.

In the eye of the storm,

I dance until my soul

Splinters against your thunder.

Haloed by sun, we shatter

And dissolve

Until we become less than breath.

Beloved, press my fruit to your hunger

So I may bleed my ecstasy

And offer my divinity,

For this hour,

If only this hour, I am immortal.

Circle

You have pressed your life
To mine before;
Your eyes are not new,
Eyes that startle me
In the night with remembrance.
Your soul is still a trembling wick
At the end of a star, and your smile is still
The sun's wandering brother.
I would still ransom tomorrow
For your kiss in the rain
Or to be a wind-tossed leaf
That blows across your path
On your journey back to me.

Eden-Heart

I have tended this garden,

This Eden-heart for four decades,

Ripped poison roots

From beds of dreams

And pruned back to nothing

To make way for the wine.

I have shred my words on thorns

For a single taste of fruit

And nursed meadows of inspiration

Until they burst into song.

I have tended a single bloom

From infancy,

Extraordinary, one of a kind,

Haunted by its fragrance in the night,

Certain I will not outlive it.

And now, this flower, here at my feet,

One of which I have no knowledge…

This cup of fire

Scorches the bone,

And I long to touch

Its forbidden center.

Adam passing through,

Brilliant and gleaming,

Untouchable,

And it is enough.

Wind's Turning

I thought I saw you,

Barely touched by the years.

Three steps behind you

In the deafening crowd

I thought I saw you.

Would you have known me

Beneath this painted mask of time?

Would your heart have remembered,

If only for a second,

Like a jewel of sun on water

That glimmers and glints

And then is gone

With the wind's turning?

Eos

Just beneath the surface of sleep,

Your smile tastes like sunlight

And your soul is full with morning.

Come to me, angel of the hours,

Into the temple of my heart

That holds the altar of your beauty,

The book of your eyes.

Beneath the surface of waking,

Before this life,

I gave you the key to my nights

And my shattering.

Open me, angel of the dawn,

Open me.

Incense

Beneath your fire, I am incense

Gathered, prepared,

Bitter resin

That burns in sweetness only once.

O, release me

From this dark box of time,

Reserved not for a saint or a deity

But for your burning eyes,

Holy, honored guest of my soul…

Beloved alchemist,

Turn the bitterness of this life

Into fragrance and burn me well.

Burn me well.

Bitter Fruit

Stillborn

Like the others,

I carried this dream

Year after year

Through decades of fear

Not enough earth

Too many graves to dig

No space for yet another

O, let it be, let it rest

No purpose

For milk in the breast

Let it be, let it rest

No purpose

For love in the breast

Blood Muse

From a shadow across your cheek

I sheltered a thousand dreams.

From the dust of your dance

I built a civilization of ideals.

From the sun in your eyes

I painted the grace of God.

From your indifference

I composed a rage

That taught the thunder.

From the sword

Of your touch never given

I gutted my own soul.

From your heart's shallow cup

I burned in famine.

Dark heart, there are no more hopes,

No more nights,

No more lessons to learn

Except how to close the book.

Black Ribbon

I do not remember

The exact day we died,

But I remember

You were wearing

A light blue shirt

And the wings in your eyes

That once carried me home

Were broken.

I searched the man

In the light blue shirt

For the lost fire,

But all I found

Was morning sun

Resting on two cold hearts.

Today,

We live separate realities,

But somewhere,

We still walk together

Unburdened by impossible dreams.

Somewhere we live

Out the future

We risked everything for

That never happened.

The last time it rained

I saw us run by

Beneath an umbrella;

We danced to our song

That played on the radio

Last night on my way home.

We haunt beaches

And rose gardens,

Unaware of the black ribbon

Pressed to our photograph

At the bottom

Of a remembrance box.

Ten Years

After a decade, a glimpse of you

Your face turned,

My heart still not safe

From memories blooming

In forgotten soil.

A glimpse, your back turned,

And I remember never holding you;

A glimpse

And I am young again,

So young I believe

My single touch

Could dissolve your stone.

Requiem

Defeated, the sun goes down,

Wounded and bleeding scarlet

On the cold battlefield of the west.

I mourn its passing,

But who mourns for you,

You who have left my life?

No one else attends this mass,

Only memories

Cloaked and candled in the dusk

Around the dust

Of who you once were.

Ember of my first fire,

Tear of my first sorrow,

I search your ashes for a well

To quench the virgin desire

Still sparking in the night.

Singer of silence, I listen

For your second-coming,

But you left my life as you entered it,

A soundless star scarring the earth with

Frigid heat.

Beautiful ghost,

You hold the heart of my youth

And the wound you made.

I still tremble for the love you,

The pain of you,

The chasm of lives

Never to be mended.

The years have left scars;

And my soul is bitter fruit.

What a strange harmony,

Love and hate,

And how the child who loved you

Still struggles to remember

The words to an unfinished song.

Goodnight, goodbye my friend.

I leave you lilies

If you should ever glance backward.

Winter Garden

After a thousand dreams,

I am here again in your light.

After a thousand dreams,

Pain dies against your smile,

The deep pulse of dawn

I cannot taste;

I cannot touch;

I cannot own.

(The garden wears winter,

Unaware of this season of fire.)

After a thousand dreams,

I am here again in your darkness.

After a thousand dreams,

The pain is reborn with your smile,

The deep pulse of night

I cannot taste;

I cannot touch;

I cannot own.

Anniversary

Soft and full of miles,

You fit me with the ease

Of worn leather.

How long it has been

Since the dawn of us…

My love, you are the one

Who taught me thunder.

How good it is to feel

Your eyes reach into mine

With their old knowing,

Knowing the journey

Even before I tell it.

Sit with me

As light washes in

And finds the blue of your eye

And the line of your cheek

Rough with morning.

Sit with me

As you always do

And fold me

Against your chest;

Let us sit

As we always have

Until we are

A tangled knot

Of thoughts

And words

And breath,

Longing to find

The core of this fire.

After all is said and done,

After the end of the end,

It will be us.

Sit with me;
Rock me
Against your words,
Your voice more beautiful
Than I remember
All those years ago,
More beautiful
Than anything
Worth remembering.

Cage

My heart, wrapped in your absence

Waits…

For a breath, a smile.

In me, love's impatient wings

Thrash against the cage

Of this unending dream of miles,

And I envy even the wind

Against your cheek.

September

We walked after the rain

Into a sapphire night.

We talked about small things

We would forget by morning

And pointed to stars

Burning through clouds

That would live only an hour.

But when I am old

I will still remember

The ballet slippers I wore

Into the street and your sudden smile

When the wind blew my shawl

Against your hair.

Second Chance

It has been years

Since we blushed the moon

And shamed the stars,

Ten years

Since I remembered

How you bounce your heels

When you are impatient

And how poppy seeds

Get stuck In your teeth

And how profanity

Sounds like Shakespeare

On your tongue.

Ten years

Since I remembered

How I look at you as if

You've just created the world

And you remind me

That you didn't

And how our bodies

Split the atom

And it is still never enough;

Ten years

Since I forgot

Where I was driving

Because I was dreaming about

How you smell like honey

And how your tenderness

Jewels my senses

And how much I love

Getting mad at you

When you remind me

That you were right

All those years ago

About how much I love you,

And someday, someday,

I would remember.

Deliverance

Hunted by the wolf

And shunned by the stranger,

I clung to this foreign soil

And my bitterness grew.

On nights when tears ushered sleep,

My soul asked for you.

Rewarded silence

And sheltered by indifference,

I sought a gentler place

When storm winds blew.

On cold, quiet mornings

Waiting for sun,

My heart asked for you.

In search of words

And vineyards of truth,

I listened for those who knew.

Groping in forests of wisdom unfound,

My mind asked for you.

Shackled in solitude

And tired with thirst,

I pressed the fruit

Of fulfillment in vain.

When ecstasy withdrew

From my futile grasp,

My body asked for you.

Mosaic

Between blind chrysalis

And triumphant wing,

Between the stupor

Of disillusionment

And the sobriety of answered prayer,

I waited for your footsteps.

You came during the darkest night

Of the soul,

Your smile a small dawn.

Mosaic of morning inlaid with light,

I welcome you,

Trembling with awakening.

Fire Flight

My heart

On the precipice of you

Sunrise burning the edge

The taste of a thousand dawns

Beneath your tongue

The rhythm of a thousand nights

In your eyes

My heart

On the precipice of you

Out of the cage, without a net

Sudden flight into fire

Legacy

Beneath this ocean of starlight

We are a pulse

In the night's beating heart,

Milky Way spilling stars

Through the ages

Blessing centuries of raptures.

The night is ancient and will pardon

Our youth and this idleness.

Tonight, there are no books to write,

Miles to exhaust,

Or hungers to satiate;

Only love must be attended to.

The night is ancient

And we touch on sands

That hold the bones of our elders,

Lovers, all of them,

And it is love they remember;

It is the only thing.

Last Touch

5:30 a.m.

Dawn comes in whispering light
Ten minutes before the alarm
I stir into his arms
In the half light,
Eyes closed
I know him by heart,
Know the scent
Of moss and honey
Just where his hair curls
At the base of his neck.
I know him by heart,
The citadel of chest
And soft cheek;
I know us by heart,
The soft intersection

Of thigh and knee,

The effortless tangle of half-sleep

And "I love you,"

The song of morning's half-light.

Eden

This terrain, rugged and smooth
Earth and wind, water and ember
This new continent
Formed by lava and sea
Moving as if with glacier magnitude
His body

Compact and certain
In his grace and his heartbeat
This terrain is familiar and wild
Soft meadows of sleep
Thunder and darkness
All that he is beneath my reverence

Last Touch

Another spring night descends

With wings of rain and remembrance.

Somewhere, you listen,

Waiting for my return.

For a moment, I hear your heartbeat

On the wind;

Sweetness drifts in through

The half-open door,

And you send one last touch to me.

Twilight

Peaceful twilight
Neither day nor night,
Thy heaven's still,
Neither dark nor light.

Silver moon,
Crescent in the west,
Cast thy beams upon my breast;
Lighten the corridors of my heart
With his infinite song.
Take the sunlight from his shoulder
And create my spirit's dawn.

Sleeping Endymion

Shadows of the winds

Dance across your sleeping eyes,

The light, a chisel

Sculpting your being.

But who holds

The instrument that creates you?

Who is so great, so beautiful

To bring you forth?

Surely, you are God's masterpiece.

I love you, I whisper.

Tonight, unafraid, facing the wind,

I love you.

Phoenix

Here the heart's journey ends

Here

Infinite search

Becomes Fruition

Here

The journey ends

In this bed of fire

We rise again

Phoenix lovers blazing

With the sky on our backs

Pardon

Snow falls in whispered constancy,

Pardoning the world

And its soiled heart,

Falling in whispered prayer

As you gaze out a window

In your half-buttoned white.

Beautiful friend,

Your soul steals my breath,

Your soul, soft as the light

Across your breast,

Soft as snow falling in white whisper

Beyond the window.

I have known your eyes

For seventeen winters
Yet today they are new,
New as the year and the world
In this pardon of white.

Beautiful man,
I have traveled the world
And its soiled heart
To find you in this heaven light,
The rain of silver prayer
As you gaze out a window
In your half-buttoned white.

You are so new, fragile glass
In this awakening,
This soft shattering.
Snow falls
And so, too, this heart,

Blooming, breaking,

If you will have me,

If only for this hour of pardon.

Soul Memory

I have never known

Your arms

Yet they have held

Me for lifetimes.

I have never

Witnessed morning

In your eyes,

Yet I have studied your face

In a hundred dawns.

You are so new

Your voice is not yet

Distilled into memory,

Yet I hear your words

In my own heart's beating.

You have not been here

Long enough

For me to grieve

Your absence,

Yet before sleep,

I whisper

Your name in tears.

First Winter

Flicker of winter candle

Midnight and steady snow

Our bed with the chocolate sheets

And the cradle of your arms

Hour upon hour

Your dreaming warmth

Against all of me

Half-sleep, turning toward

Your whisper, "I love you so…"

Blue morning and the taste of coffee

Beneath your tongue

And your open shirt

Like the sustenance of warm bread

Storm's End

We linger across ancient cobblestone
Our footfalls lost in the centuries.
We cry against morning's gray heart.
Bound in stone, an angel looks on,
Dispassionate without
The sun's illusion.
The sky breaks its vessel of rain;
We run beneath a doorway,
Warm mouth against warm mouth,
Shoulders dappled with tears.
Cobblestone glistens like agate,
Morning leans toward noon,
Sunburst.
Terra cotta landscape
Dreams in apricot.

In a deserted courtyard,

I am in your arms,

Music drifting

From a second story window.

Vow

Today, I give you my heart,

Relinquishing all fear of tomorrow.

Today, I give you my trust,

Discarding all doubt.

Today, I give you my dreams

So they may nourish

Your hungry hours.

Today, I give you my faith

So I may know God with you.

Today, I give you my love

So I may be a better person

By loving you.

Today, I give you my body

So it may be an instrument

Of my love.

Today, I give you all the selves

I have been,

The self I am now,

And the selves I will be.

I give you my hand

So we may dance through life

In laughter and in tears,

In bounty and in deprivation,

In continuity and in change,

All the days of my life.

The End

We walk a gray autumn beach

Wearing old conversations

Long outgrown.

Tireless, the arms of the sea

Reach

'Round clusters

Of mossy stone.

I lean my head

In your hands…

We can't go forward.

We can't go back.

We can't stand still.

As the sea

Whitens the sand

We cover old topics,

Laugh and pretend,
And then fall silent;
No use to go on,
We've reached the end.

Canticle:
A Modern Song of Solomon

He is beloved, Friend, Lover;

There are worlds

Beneath his tongue,

Liquid sun,

Ember nights.

He is humble as the soil;

Like roots invisible,

At first glance,

Deep and tangled with wisdom.

He is quiet sustenance,

Wild and spinning prayer.

There is song

In the shadows of his face

And a canticle

Of dawn

In his eyes.

In the close-curtained reverie

Of my thoughts,

I recite the litany

Of his being.

He is only a man;

I am only a woman

Clothed in the miracle

Of his smile.

My desire burns

On the ocean

Of this love,

A flame without wick,

Without end;
It is an invisible sun
That will live
When my flesh is no longer his
And his flesh is no longer mine.

I dip my breasts into morning
And his mouth
Fills with daybreak.
His breath is pomegranate;
His body, honey and storm,
And I am drenched
With satiety.

He is husband, my soul-divided.
He is the wealth
Of all my days,
And each hour spent

In his dappled light

Endows my eternity.

Trinity

The sleeping heart is empty,
The awakened is glad,
The wounded is wise.

But we must know each–
The sleeping, the awakened,
And the wounded–
Before we can say
We have truly loved.

Index to First Lines

A child's laughter......73

A white wall......114

After a decade, a 136

After a thousand dreams......140

Along a pathway of moon......55

Another spring night......160

At dream's end......108

Beneath the night's starry......120

Beneath this ocean of starlight......154

Beneath your fire......128

Between blind chrysalis......152

Blue smoke morning......11

City dawn, a gray flower......84

Dark moon, deep kiss......59

Dawn comes in......157

Day emerges......51

Day of thorns......96

Defeated, the sun goes down......137

Desire like an open 6

Dream me awake......100

Drumming in the streets......31

First taste of wanting......70

Flicker of winter candle......169

From a shadow......131

He brushes past me......91

He is beloved, Friend, Lover......176

He moves inside me......54

Heart famished......16

Here the heart's journey ends......163

Hunted by the wolf......150

I did not know......83

I do not remember the exact......133

I feel the cloak of your arms......20

I have eaten at your table......99

I have never known......167

I have tended this garden......124

I imagine myself......69

I look into eyes......17

I thought I saw you......126

I wake to the sound......79

I would die for you......18

In the wake of burning......38

In you, new harvest......81

It has been years......147

Just beneath the surface......127

Laughter across the way......106

Laughter overflows......50

Like the others......130

Lover, press my petals......121

Mist like ash......65

Morning, an hour old......78

My heart on the......153

My heart, wrapped in your......145

Night wind......62

On a night that lifts your eyes......103

Our bodies wear the waves......9

Our laughter drifts......71

Our words flutter......93

Outside, the wind......116

Peaceful twilight......161

Reason to ruin, senses drugged......60

Shadows of the winds......162

She sits three benches away......75

Silhouetted against city light......63

Sixteen seasons of cold......13

Sleep, savior to the wound......41

Slow dance to Spanish music......64

Snow falls......164

So this is what it would be like......52

Soft and full of miles......142

Solstice moon, holy and heavy......88

Stranger with eyes......33

Sunrise, the virgin......117

The day is like warm clay......112

The fire's gold hunger......34

The rain's cool breath......47

The sea shimmers......36

The sleeping heart is empty......180

The waves are wild tonight......85

This night, a leaf in amber......39

This terrain, rugged......161

Thou hast pierced me......89

Today, I give you my heart......172

Twilight shakes blue petals......28

Wash my soul......66

We linger across ancient......172

We sat near the street......86

We sit in your car......114

We take the path......25

We walk a gray autumn......174

We walk to the rhythm......102

We walked after the rain......146

We whisper, afraid a single......67

Where October drifts by......7

Wind and reed entwine......119

With my heart's wine......109

With one glimpse of your eyes......98

Within each soul......111

You are so much nearer......29

You began a drop of rain......22

You drink the night......14

You have pressed your life......123

You walked in carrying......104

You writhe in the dance......23

Your black boots......57

Your child......97

About the Author

Marlaina Donato is the author of several books including the poetry volumes **A Brief Infinity** and **Alabaster** as well as the titles **Spiritual Famine in the Age of Plenty** and **Broken Jar**. She is also a multimedia artist.

She and her beloved husband Joe live in beautiful rural New Jersey. To learn more about her books or to peruse her online visual art galleries, please visit: www.booksandbrush.net

www.ingramcontent.com/pod-product-compliance
Lightning Source LLC
Chambersburg PA
CBHW031317040426
42443CB00005B/116